sufo

RECIPES FROM

South-West
FRANCE

SOUTH-WEST FRANCE – INDEX

C O N T E N T S

CHOCOLATE AND MACAROON CHARLOTTE

St Emilion au chocolat

 Preparation 45 minutes   Refrigerate overnight

Serves 8

40 medium-size macaroons, approximately, for a 1½-quart charlotte mold

5 tablespoons Cognac

5 tablespoons water

For the filling:

¾ cup (1½ sticks) softened butter

1 cup superfine sugar

10 ounces bittersweet chocolate, broken into small pieces

¾ cup milk

2 medium-size egg yolks

Make the filling first. Combine the butter and sugar until creamy and smooth.

Melt the chocolate in a pan over boiling water.

In the meantime, in a small pan, bring the milk to a boil, and keep warm. When the chocolate is melted, stir with a wooden spoon until the mixture is creamy.

Then gradually pour in the hot milk, stirring all the time. Leave to cool for 3 to 5 minutes, then beat in the egg yolks.

When completely cool, beat the chocolate mixture into the creamed butter and sugar. Mix well until it becomes lighter in color.

Butter the charlotte mold. In a small bowl, mix the Cognac and water and quickly dip each macaroon into the mixture, coating both sides.

Place a first layer of dipped macaroons in the base of the mold, flat-side down. Then build 2 rows up the sides of the mold, flat-side out. Spoon half the chocolate cream into the mold, then place a layer of dipped macaroons on top, flat-side down. Then fill with the rest of the chocolate cream. Cover with a final layer of dipped macaroons flat-side up.

Cover with a weighted plate and put in the refrigerator overnight.

The following day, place the bottom of the mold in a bowl of hot water for a few seconds, then turn out the charlotte straight away onto a dish and serve immediately.

SOUTH-WEST FRANCE

French cuisine has been highly regarded throughout the world for many, many years and even today, in the ever-evolving world kitchen, it is still thought of as one of the leading forces in cookery. French cuisine, however, is a generic term, especially as each region within France boasts its own distinct style of cooking, flavors and ingredients. But what is true of French cooking as a whole is that traditions have been preserved religiously in the French kitchen and many dishes that form the backbone of French cuisine today can be dated back many centuries.

Most of the recipes that have been chosen for this book are great classics from South-West France, a region rich in culinary tradition and local produce.

These recipes have been thoroughly researched, sometimes simplified, lightened, or adapted to today's taste and way of life, and then carefully tested and "tasted." The ingredients have also been researched for availability, and alternatives are suggested where necessary, while still retaining the taste and authenticity of the recipes.

The South-West, known in France as the Sud-Ouest, stretches from the Périgord in the north to the Pyrenees in the south, and from the Landes and Gascony in the west to the Languedoc in the east. It is a vast area of France that also encompasses many smaller regions, each with its own distinct style of cooking.

In general terms, the South-West can be gastronomically defined by confits – an age-old tradition of preserving goose, duck, or pork in its own fat; foie gras, which is produced in several regions of the South-West; and goose fat, a very important ingredient in the cooking of this area, although it can often be replaced by butter, as suggested in some of the recipes in this book.

However, the flavors of South-West France are also based on many regional specialties.

From Périgord come the famous black truffles, the chestnuts, and the walnuts, which are used in both sweet and savory dishes. Walnuts are pressed to make a strong-flavored oil, delicious in salad dressings.

The Quercy is south of Périgord, and is the land of melons, apricots, peaches, and prunes, the latter of which are dried and sold as the famous pruneaux d'Agen. It is also renowned for the dark-colored wine produced in Cahors, called Vin de Cahors.

Further south-east is the Languedoc region and the town of Toulouse, famous for its sausage. This is the land of the cassoulet – a bean stew enriched with meat, sausage, and pieces of goose confit.

To the north-west is the Bordelais. Bordeaux is famous for its wines. It is also where the best cèpes (wild mushrooms) can be found.

Traveling south-east from Bordeaux, there is Gascony which provides some of the best poultry in France and the famous spirit, Armagnac, which is aged in oak for several years and is one of the world's best brandies. Armagnac is also wonderful to cook with and is often added to desserts.

To the west of Gascony and along the Atlantic coast is a sandy land of swamps and pine forests called the Landes, where the most delicate foie gras is produced and the famous blue-veined cheese made with ewe's milk – Roquefort.

The most southerly region, the Basque country, enjoys yet another distinct

cuisine, enlivened by the piment d'Espelette, a hot red pepper added to many dishes such as Pipérade (a mixture of eggs, tomatoes, peppers, and onions) and to the Ttoro, a Basque fish soup. It is here too, in the town of Bayonne, by the Atlantic coast, that the famous Bayonne ham is produced.

But these are just a few of the classic dishes of South-West France. So, go ahead and indulge yourself in these recipes. Recreate in your kitchen the wonderful flavors of this unique region.

PASTRY FRITTERS
Merveilles

Preparation
30 minutes

Cooking
20 minutes

Serves 6

2 good cups all-purpose flour

½ teaspoon baking powder

3 medium-size eggs

4 tablespoons softened butter

1 tablespoon superfine sugar

1 pinch salt

Zest of 2 lemons, grated

Confectioners' sugar

Vegetable oil for frying

Sift the flour and baking powder into a bowl. Make a well in the center, add the eggs, butter, sugar, salt, and lemon zest. Knead gently with your hands into a smooth dough. Wrap it in foil and refrigerate for 30 minutes.

Roll out the dough to ⅛ inch thick and cut into 3-inch x 1-inch strips.

Heat the oil in a pan and when quite hot, fry the strips. They will puff up and brown very quickly. Turn once and remove with a slotted spoon.

Dry them on paper towels, dust with confectioners' sugar and they are ready to serve.

They are delicious hot or cold.

BASQUE FISH SOUP
Ttoro

⏰ Preparation 10 minutes | Refrigerate overnight
🕐 Cooking 1 hour | Serves 6

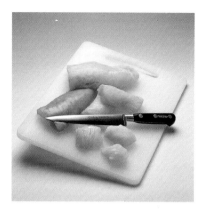

This soup was originally made by the fishermen of St Jean-de-Luz, in the Basque region, with the most inexpensive fish. Nowadays, however, it is enriched with shellfish, monkfish and eel. The addition of dried chili gives it a typical Basque flavor.

For the fish stock:

2½ pounds fish trimmings and bones, including fish heads of cod, scrod, or haddock

¼ cup olive oil

2 medium-size onions, thinly sliced

2 garlic cloves, crushed

2 large tomatoes, peeled (see page 24), seeded, and chopped

1¼ cups dry white wine

Bouquet garni: thyme, parsley, and bay leaf

1 medium-size dried red chili, crushed

3¾ cups water

For the soup:

2 pounds mixed fish fillets, such as halibut, monkfish, cod, and red mullet

All-purpose flour

Salt and freshly ground pepper

⅓ cup olive oil

1 pound raw mussels, cleaned and scrubbed

6 raw langoustines or extra large prawns

To make the fish stock, heat the olive oil and sauté the onions, garlic, fish heads, and trimmings. When the onions start to brown, add the tomatoes, white wine, bouquet garni, chili, and water.

Bring to a boil, cover the pan, and simmer gently for 45 minutes, stirring occasionally.

Pour through a fine strainer, pressing with a wooden spoon. Return the liquid to a clean pan and discard the rest.

To make the soup, cut the fish into large pieces and roll them in the flour seasoned with salt and pepper.

Heat the oil in a large non-stick skillet. Shake the excess flour from the pieces of fish, and sauté them for about 2 minutes on each side.

Remove from the oil and arrange in the bottom of a large heavy casserole. Add the mussels, and langoustines or prawns. Bring the reserved fish stock to a boil and pour over the fish in the casserole. Cover and cook gently over low heat for about 7 minutes, or until the mussels have opened.

Sprinkle with chopped parsley and serve, taking care not to break up the pieces of fish.

ORANGE TART
Tarte à l'orange

Preparation 30 minutes   Refrigerate 2 hours

Cooking 35 minutes   Serves 6 to 8

For the pastry:

1⅓ cups all-purpose flour

1 medium-size egg

½ cup (1 stick) softened butter

¼ cup superfine sugar

Pinch salt

About ¼ cup water

For the filling:

4 medium-size eggs

1 scant cup superfine sugar

Grated zest of 5 oranges

1¼ cups fresh orange juice

⅔ cup (1¼ stick) butter

Butter a deep 11-inch tart pan.

Prepare the short pastry dough either by hand or in a food processor.

If made by hand, put the flour in a bowl. Make a well in the center, add the egg, the butter, sugar, salt, and water.

Knead gently with your hands until you obtain a smooth dough, adding a little more water if the mixture is too dry. If made in a food processor, process first the flour, butter, sugar, and salt quickly together, then add the egg and water through the funnel and process until the

dough forms a ball around the blade.

Wrap the dough in foil and leave it to rest in the refrigerator for 1 to 2 hours.

Roll out the dough on a floured base and line the tart pan with it.

To make the filling, beat the eggs in a bowl, then gradually add the sugar, beating all the time, until frothy and pale. Add the grated zest and the orange juice and mix well.

Preheat the oven to 400°F.

Slowly melt the butter and gradually stir it into the egg and orange mixture. Mix well and pour onto the uncooked dough. Only fill ⅔ of the tart pan, otherwise it will overflow during baking.

Bake the tart for 25 to 35 minutes, until the mixture is set and the surface is golden-brown.

Decorate the top of the tart with strands of orange zest to serve.

GARLIC SOUP
Tourain

Preparation
5 minutes

Cooking
50 minutes   Serves 4

You can omit the egg whites from the recipe and use them to make meringues, for example.

2 tablespoons goose fat or butter

12 fresh garlic cloves, peeled

6¼ cups chicken stock

Bouquet garni: sprigs of thyme, sage, and 2 bay leaves, tied together

Salt and freshly ground pepper

3 medium-size eggs

1 cup grated Emmenthal or Gruyère cheese

4 slices of white bread, toasted

Melt the fat or butter in a large soup pan. Add the whole garlic cloves and sweat them over low heat until they turn a light golden color, taking care not to burn them.

Gradually pour the stock into the pan, add the bouquet garni, salt and pepper to taste, and give it a stir. Return to a boil, cover, and simmer over low heat for about 30 minutes.

Remove the soup from the heat and let it cool for 10 minutes. Remove the bouquet garni. Transfer to a blender or food processor and purée for a few seconds until the soup is smooth.

Return to the soup pan. Separate the eggs and beat the egg whites until foamy. Pour them slowly into the hot soup, gently beating all the time, and let the egg whites cook for 1 minute or so, still beating.

Put the egg yolks in a small bowl, and very slowly pour two ladles of hot soup onto the yolks, stirring constantly. Then pour the mixture back into the soup, and allow to thicken over very low heat for 3 to 4 minutes, stirring constantly. Do not allow to boil, or the soup will curdle.

Place whole slices of toasted bread into individual soup plates, sprinkle the grated cheese on top, and pour the soup over.

WINE AND HONEY CREME CARAMEL

Crème caramel au vin et au miel

Preparation 20 minutes

Cooking 40 minutes

Serves 6

2¼ cups sweet white wine

⅔ cup clear honey

1 good pinch of cinnamon, or 1 cinnamon stick

2 strips of lemon peel

4 whole medium-size eggs

2 medium-size egg yolks

⅓ cup water

½ cup superfine sugar

In a small pan, gently simmer the wine, honey, cinnamon, and lemon peel for about 10 minutes. Then, leave to cool a little.

Meanwhile, beat together the 4 whole eggs and the 2 egg yolks, then very slowly pour the wine mixture onto the eggs, beating all the time.

In a thick-based saucepan, mix the water and sugar, bring slowly to a boil, stirring until the sugar has melted completely. Then let it boil, without stirring, until it turns a light brown. Take off the heat immediately and pour this caramel into a 1-quart baking dish, or 6 individual ramekins, swirling the dish (or ramekins) around, so that the bottom and sides are coated with caramel.

Preheat the oven to 325°F.

Pour the honey and egg mixture into the dish (or individual ramekins) and cook in a bain-marie, in the oven, for 35 to 40 minutes for a baking dish, and 25 to 30 minutes for individual ramekins, taking care not to overcook.

Leave to cool and keep in the refrigerator until ready to serve.

To serve, unmold onto a dish deep enough to take the liquid caramel that will run down the sides of the crème caramel.

PEA AND SORREL SOUP
La soupe aux petits pois et à l'oseille

Preparation
20 minutes

Cooking
55 minutes

Serves 4

Fresh peas are seasonal. You can use frozen peas for this soup, but the taste will be different and they need less cooking time.

3 tablespoons goose fat or butter

1 pound fresh peas, shelled

2 tablespoons all-purpose flour

4¼ cups beef or chicken stock

Salt and freshly ground pepper

8 scallions, chopped

2 garlic cloves, chopped

1 handful of sorrel

1 medium-size egg yolk

In a large soup pan, gently melt 2 tablespoons of the fat or butter, then add the peas, and turn them in the fat to coat them.

Sprinkle the peas with the flour and let it cook for 1 to 2 minutes. Gradually stir in the stock and season to taste. Add the scallions and garlic, cover, and simmer gently for approximately 45 minutes.

Meanwhile, wash the sorrel, drain, remove the stalks, and chop into thin strips with a sharp knife. In a small skillet, melt the remaining fat or butter, and very gently sauté the sorrel strips for 1 minute, then set aside.

Remove the soup from the heat and purée in a blender or food processor until smooth. Pour it back into the soup pan, add the fried strips of sorrel, and gently reheat for 2 minutes.

In a small bowl, beat the egg yolk and slowly stir in a ladle of the hot soup, gently beating all the time to stop the yolk from curdling. Then pour it all back into the soup and, stirring all the time, let it thicken over low heat for about 2 to 3 minutes.

WALNUT TARTLETS
Tartelettes aux noix

 Preparation
45 minutes

Refrigerate
1 hour

Cooking
35 minutes

Serves 6

1½ cups all-purpose flour

½ cup (1 stick) softened butter

¼ cup superfine sugar

2 to 3 tablespoons water

1 medium-size egg yolk

For the filling:

½ cup milk

½ cup heavy cream + (optional) 2 tablespoons heavy cream

1 cup sugar

⅓ cup water

2 cups coarsely chopped walnuts

Confectioners' sugar

Place the flour in a large mixing bowl. Make a well in the center and add the butter, sugar, water, and egg yolk. Mix the ingredients together with your fingertips until you have a smooth dough. Knead the dough into a ball, wrap in foil or plastic, and put in the refrigerator for 1 hour.

Preheat the oven to 425°F.

On a floured base, roll out the dough and line six 4-inch tart pans. Prick the dough with a fork. Make collars with foil to cover the sides of each tartlet and bake blind for 15 to 18 minutes, until cooked. Take them out of the oven and let them cool.

To make the filling, mix the milk and the ½ cup heavy cream in a pan, place over high heat, and bring to a boil. Reduce the heat and keep it simmering.

Put the sugar in a small pan with ⅓ cup of water over high heat. Let the sugar melt and, without stirring, continue cooking until it turns a light caramel-brown. Take care not to overcook !

Over medium-low heat, add a little of the hot milk and cream mixture to the caramel. Wait until the bubbling stops, then pour in the rest. You may use a sugar thermometer and continue to cook, stirring occasionally with the thermometer, until it registers 225°F. Or, if you are not using a thermometer, cook for 5 to 8 minutes, stirring from time to time. You can add 2 tablespoons of cream, if desired, which will improve the texture.

Place the walnuts in a bowl, pour the caramel mixture over them, and swirl the bowl to coat

all the walnuts. Dust the edges of the tartlets with confectioners' sugar, and fill each one with the walnut mixture.

Allow them to cool and serve.

PUMPKIN SOUP
La soupe à la citrouille

Pumpkin can be used in soups, stews, in sweet pies, or just as a vegetable, mashed with lots of butter and pepper. You can also cook the seeds: spread on a baking sheet, sprinkle with salt, and bake in a moderate oven for about 20 minutes. Serve with aperitifs.

1 large onion, chopped

1 tablespoon goose fat, pork fat, or butter

2 large ripe tomatoes, peeled (see page 24), seeded, and chopped

3 garlic cloves, crushed

Bouquet garni: thyme, parsley, and bay leaf

2 cups peeled and diced potatoes

1½ pounds pumpkin, peeled, seeded, and cubed

6¼ cups water

Salt and freshly ground pepper

1 tablespoon chopped fresh chives

Fry the onion gently in the goose or pork fat in a soup pan for about 5 minutes.

Add the tomatoes, garlic, and bouquet garni. Cover and cook gently for a further 5 minutes.

Add the potatoes, pumpkin, water, and salt and pepper to taste.

Bring the soup to a boil, cover, and simmer for 45 minutes, stirring occasionally. The pumpkin cubes should soften but not break up.

Sprinkle the chopped chives on the top before serving.

CREAM OF CHESTNUT SOUP
Le potage aux marrons à la crème

1 pound fresh chestnuts, peeled (see page 24)
or
1 pound canned/vacuum – packed chestnuts

1 tablespoon goose fat or butter

1 medium-size onion, chopped

1 celery stalk, chopped

1 large garlic clove, chopped

4¼ cups chicken stock

2 cups milk

Salt and freshly ground pepper

4 tablespoons heavy cream, crème fraîche, or sour cream

In a soup pan, heat the goose fat or butter and gently sauté the onion, celery, and garlic. Then add the chestnuts, stock, milk, salt and pepper. Stir and bring slowly to a boil. Cover and simmer for 45 minutes (25 to 30 minutes if you are using canned or vacuum-packed chestnuts).

Remove the soup from the heat and purée in a blender or food processor until smooth. Pour it back into the soup pan and

reheat gently.

If the soup is too thick, add a little stock or milk to thin it.

Serve in individual soup plates, with a tablespoon of heavy cream, crème fraîche, or sour cream swirled on top.

PRUNE SOUFFLE
Soufflé aux pruneaux

Preparation
10 minutes

Soak
overnight

Cooking
55 minutes

Serves 6

About 1½ cups pitted prunes

1 cup superfine sugar

Juice of 1 lemon

6 large egg whites

Soak the prunes overnight. Then cook them gently in enough water to cover them for about 10 minutes, until tender. Drain and blend them to a purée.

Add the sugar and lemon juice to the purée and stir well.

Butter a 1-quart soufflé dish (or 6 individual ramekins) and dust with sugar.

Beat the egg whites until stiff and fold into the prune purée.

Preheat the oven to 375°F.

Pour the prune mixture into the buttered dish(es), and bake in the center of the oven for 45 minutes for a soufflé dish, and 30 minutes for individual ramekins.

Serve warm or cold with cream.

LIMA BEAN SOUP
Le potage aux fèves

Preparation
30 minutes

Cooking
15 minutes

Serves 6

Savoury (sariette), the herb, is often used with lima beans in soups or purées - but use it with caution as it is rather strong. Here we have used parsley instead. This recipe works equally well with frozen lima beans, which means you can make this soup all year!

6 slices of large smoked sausage
or
18 slices of small smoked sausage

3 tablespoons goose fat or butter

2 medium-size onions, finely chopped

2 carrots, peeled, and finely chopped

2 garlic cloves, crushed

2 tablespoons all-purpose flour

3¾ pints chicken stock

1 pounds lima beans, shelled
or
1½ pounds frozen lima beans

2½ tablespoons chopped fresh parsley

If you are using a large smoked sausage, cut it into chunks. If you are using small smoked sausages, cut them into slices.

Fry the sausage in the goose fat or butter for approximately 3 minutes. Remove the sausage from the pan and set aside. In the same pan cook the onion, carrot, and garlic for 3 to 4 minutes. Stir in the flour and, when it has amalga-mated with the fat, add the stock little by little, stirring all the time.

Bring to a boil, add the beans and sausage, cover, turn down the heat, and simmer slowly, stirring occasionally, until the beans are tender.

Stir in the parsley, cook for a further 5 minutes, and serve.

BAKED CHERRY PUDDING
Clafoutis

Preparation
30 minutes

Cooking
45 minutes   Serves 6

1 pound black cherries	
6 tablespoons butter	
1 cup all-purpose flour	
4 medium-size eggs	
⅓ cup superfine sugar	
1 cup milk, warmed	
Confectioners' sugar to decorate	

Wash, stem and dry the cherries, but do not remove the stones.

Butter a 9-inch shallow baking dish and sprinkle with a little flour. Shake the dish to spread the flour evenly, then turn it upside-down to get rid of the excess flour.

Melt the butter in a small pan and leave to cool. Put the rest of the flour, the eggs, and sugar in a bowl, add the melted butter, and mix well.

Gradually add the warmed milk, stirring all the time, until a smooth, pancake-type batter

is obtained. **Leave it to rest for 2 hours.**

Place the cherries in the baking dish and carefully pour the batter over them.

Preheat the oven to 375°F.

Bake in the oven for 40 to 45 minutes or until set. Cool on a rack, but do not remove from the dish until it is lukewarm.

Dust with confectioners' sugar before serving.

Clafoutis is best served lukewarm, but is also nice cold.

STRAWBERRIES IN WINE
Soupe de fraises

Preparation
20 minutes

Serves 6

We use wine from Monbazillac in this recipe, but if it is unavailable, you can use any other sweet wine from southwestern France such as Barsac.

1½ pounds strawberries, hulled and cut in half	
¼ cup superfine sugar	
1 chilled bottle of sweet white wine (preferably from Monbazillac)	

Place the strawberries in a bowl and sprinkle the sugar over.

Cover and place in the refrigerator.

20 minutes before serving, pour the cold white wine over the strawberries and return to the refrigerator until ready to serve.

RED PEPPER MOUSSE
Mousse de poivrons rouges

Preparation 1 hour
Refrigerate overnight

Cooking 20 minutes
Serves 6

4 large red bell peppers, peeled (see page 24), cored, and seeded

2 tablespoons unsalted butter

1 large garlic clove

½ teaspoon fresh thyme leaves

1 tablespoon white wine vinegar

⅔ cup heavy or whipping cream, chilled

Salt and freshly ground pepper

Cayenne pepper

Slices of white bread, toasted, to serve

The day before, cut the peppers into large cubes. Melt the butter in a heavy saucepan over medium-low heat. Add the peppers, garlic, and thyme. Cover the pan and cook slowly for about 15 to 20 minutes, stirring occasionally to avoid sticking.

Add the vinegar and cook uncovered, stirring occasionally, until all the liquid has evaporated.

Pour the mixture into a blender or food processor and purée, using the on-off motion, for 20 to 30 seconds (until smooth).

Pour into a fine strainer to drain and let it cool. Then pour the mixture into a bowl and refrigerate overnight.

The next day, put a bowl and beaters in the freezer for 1 hour. Take the purée out of the refrigerator and discard any excess liquid in the bowl. Using the chilled bowl and beaters, beat the cream until stiff. Gently fold the cold pepper purée into the whipped cream. Season to taste with salt, pepper, and cayenne pepper.

Keep chilled until ready to serve. Serve with triangles of toasted bread.

APPLE PIE FROM GASCONY
Tourte Gasconne

 Preparation 1 hour   Marinate 3 hours

Cooking 45 minutes   Serves 6

2½ pounds apples, peeled, cored, and sliced

⅔ cup Armagnac

5 tablespoons vanilla sugar

½ teaspoon orange-flower water

14 ounces prepared puff pastry dough

1 medium-size egg, beaten

Confectioners' sugar

Place the apple slices in a bowl and pour in the Armagnac. Add the vanilla sugar and orange-flower water and leave to macerate, covered, for 2 to 3 hours.

Roll out the pastry dough into 2 rounds and line a 8- to 9-inch pie pan with one round.

Drain the apple slices, reserving the Armagnac mixture. Spoon the apples on to the pastry dough.

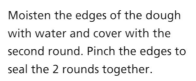

Moisten the edges of the dough with water and cover with the second round. Pinch the edges to seal the 2 rounds together.

Make a hole in the center of the pie top and make pastry leaves from leftover strips of dough. Moisten the leaves with a little water and arrange the leaves around the hole.

Place the pie in the refrigerator for 20 minutes. Meanwhile, put the Armagnac and sugar mixture into a pan and simmer to form a syrup. Set aside.

Preheat the oven to 350°F.

Brush the top of the pie with the beaten egg yolk to glaze and cook the pie in the oven for about 35 to 45 minutes, until the pastry is cooked and is a golden-brown color.

Remove from the oven, and pour the Armagnac syrup through the hole in the center of the pie.

Dust the top with confectioners' sugar and serve.

MUSSELS WITH ALMONDS
Moules farçies aux amandes

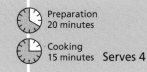

Preparation
20 minutes

Cooking
15 minutes   Serves 4

This recipe also works well with littleneck or cherrystone clams instead of mussels.

2 pounds mussels

1 cup fresh white bread crumbs (see page 25)

½ cup finely chopped or ground almonds

1 tablespoon finely chopped fresh parsley

1 large garlic clove, finely chopped

Salt and freshly ground pepper

¾ cup (1½ sticks) unsalted butter

1 stick French bread, to serve

Scrape and clean the mussels under a running tap and remove the beards. Place the mussels in a large pan with 1 cup water and steam, covered, over high heat, for about 6 to 8 minutes, or until they have opened. Take off the heat immediately. Strain, cool, and after removing the top shells, divide the mussels between 4 ovenproof dishes.

Mix the bread crumbs, almonds, parsley, garlic, salt and pepper,

and sprinkle a little of the mixture over each mussel.

Preheat the oven to 400°F.

Very gently heat the butter in a pan and spoon over the mussels. Place in a hot oven for about 5 to 7 minutes, until heated through and sizzling.

Serve with French bread to mop up the garlic butter.

ANCHOVY AND BLACK OLIVE DIP
Anchoiade

Preparation   Marinate
20 minutes   2 hours

Serves 6   Refrigerate
24 hours

This is the Languedoc version of the black olive-based tapenade found in Provence. Anchoiade uses proportionately more anchovies than black olives.

20 pitted black olives

Olive oil

3 garlic cloves, cut in thin slices

2-ounce can anchovy fillets in oil

1 tablespoon Dijon-style mustard, or similar

1 medium-size egg yolk

⅔ cup olive oil

1 tablespoon fresh lemon juice

Cayenne pepper

Slices of white bread, toasted, to serve

Marinate the black olives in olive oil (enough to just cover the olives) and the slices of garlic for at least 2 hours.

Drain the anchovy fillets and pat them dry with paper towels.

Drain the olives and place them in a blender or food processor with the anchovies and mustard. Using the on-off motion, chop

until the mixture is coarse.

Add the egg yolk and blend until smooth, slowly and steadily adding the olive oil, then the lemon juice. Add cayenne pepper to taste. Pour into a bowl and keep refrigerated for at least 24 hours.

Serve with pieces of toasted bread.

PRUNE AND ARMAGNAC ICE CREAM
Glace aux pruneaux à l'Armagnac

| Preparation 30 minutes | Soaking 6 hours |
| Cooking 10 minutes | Serves 6 |

1 good cup large pitted prunes

¾ cup Armagnac

8 large eggs

1 cup superfine sugar

4¼ cups milk

Soak the prunes in Armagnac overnight. The following day, drain the prunes, chop them coarsely, and set aside in a bowl.

Put the eggs and half the sugar in a bowl and beat until pale and creamy.

Put the rest of the sugar in a pan, add the milk, and bring to a boil. Beating all the time, pour some of the hot milk onto the beaten eggs, then return the mixture to the pan and heat gently, stirring, until a custard is obtained. Do not boil or it will curdle.

Pour the custard through a fine strainer onto the prunes. Stir well and cool.

Pour the cooled custard and prunes into an ice cream machine or place in the freezer in a covered container. Remove from the freezer from time to time, stirring the mixture briskly to obtain a creamy-textured ice cream. It will take at least 6 hours for the mixture to become ice cream.

Remove from the freezer ½ hour before serving.

SALMON RILLETTES
Rillettes de saumon

Preparation 45 minutes   Refrigerate 1 day

Cooking 5 minutes   Serves 6

Traditionally rillettes is a type of pâté made with pork where the meat is shredded rather than ground or puréed. In this recipe, the pork is replaced with salmon. The rillettes can be stored for up to two weeks in the refrigerator, providing the clarified butter seal is not broken.

9 ounces salmon fillet

Salt and freshly ground pepper

1 large (or 2 small) shallots, finely chopped

2 tablespoons unsalted butter

½ cup dry white wine

½ cup (1 stick) unsalted butter, softened and cut into small cubes

¼ pound lightly smoked salmon cut in small pieces

2 tablespoons olive oil

1 teaspoon fresh lemon juice

1 medium-size egg yolk

Pinch of freshly ground nutmeg

½ to ¾ cup clarified butter (see page 25)

1 tablespoon chopped fresh dill or chives (or both) (optional)

Slices of white bread, toasted, to serve

Sprinkle the salmon fillets with ½ teaspoon salt and leave aside. After 20 to 30 minutes, dry the salmon with paper towels.

In a large saucepan, gently sauté the shallots in a knob of butter, until soft but not brown. Add the salmon to the pan in one layer, then the white wine, and cover tightly. Cook very slowly, turning the fish once, for about 3 to 4 minutes (until the fish is cooked through).

Place the fish on a plate and remove the skin and any bones. Pour the pan juices over the fish, flake the salmon with a fork, and mix well with the cooked shallots. Leave to cool for 10 to 15 minutes.

Place the softened butter, the cooled cooked salmon and shallots, and the pieces of smoked salmon in the bowl of the food processor (with plastic blade). Using the on-off motion, rapidly combine the ingredients then, with the machine running, quickly add the olive oil, lemon juice, and egg yolk. The mixture should not be reduced to a purée but remain slightly coarse.

Transfer the mixture to a bowl, add salt and pepper to taste, the ground nutmeg, and mix well. Smooth the surface with a spatula and pour the clarified butter over to seal the surface. You can add some chopped fresh

herbs, such as dill or chives or both, to the clarified butter.

Keep refrigerated for a day or two before serving, if possible.

Serve with triangles of toasted bread.

In the same skillet, fry the onions until they are transparent, and spoon these over the meat.

Preheat the oven to 325°F.

Add the rest of the beans, the tomatoes, crushed garlic, the tomato paste diluted with ⅔ cup hot water, and add enough stock and/or water reserved from cooking the beans to just cover the cassoulet. Cover and bring to a boil, then place in a low oven for about 1 hour.

Remove the pot or casserole from the oven, give the cassoulet a good stir, add the sausages, and season to taste. Return to the oven and cook for a further 1 hour.

Remove from the oven a second time. Sprinkle the bread crumbs evenly over the top of the cassoulet, and return the pot or casserole to the oven, uncovered, for a further 30 minutes, so that the crumbs form a golden crust.

This is such a substantial dish that you need only serve it with French bread, a green salad, and a robust bottle of red wine.

EGGS WITH PEPPERS AND TOMATOES
Pipérade

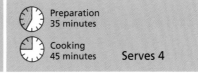

Preparation
35 minutes

Cooking
45 minutes

Serves 4

Typical of the Basque country, this dish is found throughout the region. Sometimes it is served as an omelet filled with the vegetables, or with slices of spicy sausage instead of the ham. This could make a light meal for 2, served with a green salad and crusty French bread.

3 red or green bell peppers, skinned (see p.24), cored, seeded, and diced

¼ cup olive oil

2 medium-size onions, chopped

2 large garlic cloves, finely chopped

1 fresh red or green chili pepper, seeded, and coarsely chopped
or
½ teaspoon of crushed chilies
or
¼ teaspoon cayenne pepper

1½ pounds ripe tomatoes, peeled (see p.24), seeded, and coarsely chopped

8 medium-size eggs

Salt and freshly ground pepper

1 tablespoon olive oil

4 slices of raw ham (Bayonne or Parma ham)

In a large skillet, gently heat the oil, add the onions, cover, and sweat for 5 to 10 minutes.

Add the peppers, garlic, and the chili pepper (crushed chilies or cayenne pepper). Cover the pan and cook over low heat for 10 minutes, stirring often.

Add the tomatoes and a little salt and cook, uncovered, over medium heat for 15 to 20 minutes, stirring occasionally, until the juices have evaporated.

Break the eggs in a bowl, season with salt and pepper to taste, beat lightly with a fork, and pour into the pan over the vegetables.

Cook over low heat, stirring only occasionally, until the eggs have set, but are not scrambled.

In a little more olive oil, sauté the slices of ham in a non-stick skillet for 30 to 40 seconds on each side and place on top of the eggs. Serve immediately.

CASSOULET

Preparation
1 hour

Soaking
overnight

Cooking
3 hours 30 mins Serves 8 to 10

Cassoulet is basically a bean stew enriched with pieces of meat, such as lamb, sausage, goose or duck, the proportions of which vary from region to region.

For the beans:

2 pounds white haricot beans, soaked overnight

1 large onion studded with 5 cloves

1 large carrot, cut in half

Bouquet garni of thyme, parsley, and 1 bay leaf

For the meats:

½ pound boned belly of pork in one piece

1 pound lean pork

1 pound smoked bacon

1½ pounds boned shoulder or neck fillets of lamb

⅓ cup olive oil, goose fat, or dripping

2 large onions, coarsely chopped

2 large tomatoes, peeled (see page 24), seeded and chopped

4 garlic cloves, crushed

1 large tablespoon tomato paste

⅔ cup hot water

6 to 8 Toulouse sausages or smoked sausages

Salt and freshly ground pepper

2 cups fresh bread crumbs (see page 25)

Soak the beans overnight in plenty of water.

Drain, rinse the beans, and put them in a large pan with the onion, carrot, and bouquet garni. Cover with water and bring to a boil. Cover the pan and simmer for about 45 minutes or until the beans are just tender. Do not overcook the beans.

While the beans are cooking, remove the skin from the belly of pork, reserve it, and cut the meat into cubes. Cut the lean pork into cubes. Remove the rind from the bacon. Trim any fat off the lamb and also cut into cubes.

Drain the beans, discard the onion, carrot, and bouquet garni, but reserve the cooking liquid, and set aside.

Place the piece of pork skin in the bottom of an earthenware cooking pot or large ovenproof casserole and cover with half the beans.

Heat the olive oil (or other fats) in a skillet and brown all the cubed meat and the sausages in turn. Add the meat to the beans in the pot or casserole, keeping the sausages aside.

DUCK LIVER MOUSSE
Mousse de foie de canard

Preparation
20 minutes

Marinate
2 hours

Serves 4

Refrigerate
6 hours

If it is difficult to find duck livers, this dish is every bit as delicious made with chicken livers.

1½ pounds duck livers, trimmed of skin and fat

1 cup finely diced pork fat

1 bay leaf

2 thyme sprigs

Salt and freshly ground pepper

Scant 1 cup port or brandy

6 tablespoons butter

¼ cup heavy or whipping cream

Slices of white bread, toasted, to serve

For the port jelly:

½ cup jellied chicken stock (see page 25)

3 tablespoons port or brandy

Marinate the duck livers and pork fat with the bay leaf, thyme, salt, pepper, and port or brandy, for at least 2 hours.

Remove the livers and pork fat, reserving the marinade.

Melt the butter in a pan and cook the livers for 4 to 5 minutes on each side, over medium heat, removing them from the pan while they are still pink inside. Set aside.

Cook the pork fat gently in the same pan, then add the marinade and reduce rapidly over high heat for 2 minutes.

Put the livers, fat, and reduced marinade in a food processor and reduce to a very fine purée. Add the cream, process for a further 30 seconds, check the seasoning, and pour the now mousse-like mixture into small ramekins or a terrine dish. Leave to cool.

To make the port jelly, mix the jellied chicken stock and port or brandy and reduce by about one-third over high heat. Cool, then spoon over the mousse. Cover and refrigerate for at least 6 hours or overnight.

Take the mousse out of the refrigerator at least 1 hour before serving.

Serve with triangles of toasted bread.

CONFIT OF DUCK
Confit de canard

Preparation 30 minutes	Refrigerate overnight
3 Cooking 3 hours	Serves 4 to 6

Confit is a word used to describe goose, duck, or pork which is preserved in its own fat. Although you can preserve ordinary duck, rather than the French duck from Rouen, it does not have enough of its own fat, so you have to add either canned goose fat or pork fat.

| 1 large duck |
| 3 pounds pork fat |
| or |
| Four 12-ounce cans goose fat |
| 1 tablespoon salt |
| 1 thyme sprig |
| 1 bay leaf, crumbled |
| 1 garlic clove |
| Glass jar(s) for storing |

The day before:

Cut the duck in 8 portions: cut off the legs and separate the thighs from the drumsticks by cutting through the joint.

Remove one wing and breast from the body and cut the portion in half. Repeat with the other wing and breast. Reserve any pieces of fat from the duck.

Rub the duck pieces with the salt, thyme and bay leaf. Place them in a bowl, cover, and put in the refrigerator overnight.

The following day, cut up the pork fat (if using) into small pieces and place in an ovenproof casserole or dish, adding any pieces of fat from the duck. Cover and put in a very low oven (300°F) for about 2 hours to melt the fat. If you are using canned goose fat, empty the cans into a large saucepan, adding any pieces of fat from the duck as before, and melt the fat slowly.

Rub another ovenproof casserole with garlic. Carefully wash the salt off the duck pieces under a cold tap and pat them dry with paper towels. Place them in the casserole and cover with the melted pork fat or melted goose fat.

Cover the casserole and put it in a very low oven (300°F). Cook very gently for about 2½ hours, or until very tender.

Sterilize some jars (or a large jar) by boiling them in a large pan of water for about 15 minutes, then drying them in a low oven.

Remove the pieces of duck from the casserole and pack them into the jar(s), then pour over the hot strained fat in which they have been cooking to completely cover the duck pieces. Secure the lid(s) and store in the refrigerator. This will keep in the refrigerator for

about 3 to 4 months if unopened.

Any fat left over can be stored in jars in the refrigerator, and used for other dishes such as Pommes Sarladaises (see page 19).

To serve, lift the pieces of duck out of the jar and heat in a hot oven or under a low broiler until the duck skin is crisp, about 15 minutes.

HOT SPIDER CRAB
Araignée chaude

Preparation
30 minutes

Cooking
30 minutes

Serves 4

If spider crabs are unobtainable, the dish can be made with ordinary (common) crab – or you could use frozen crab meat and put the mixture into scallop shells to make an attractive starter.

4 boiled spider crabs (about 1½ pounds each)
(or 1 pound mixed white and dark crab meat)

⅓ cup olive oil

1 leek, white part only, finely chopped

1 large onion, finely chopped

1 large carrot, finely chopped

1 celery stalk, finely chopped

½ cup dry sherry

1 pound ripe tomatoes, peeled (see page 24), seeded, and finely chopped

¼ teaspoon crushed chilies

1 tablespoon chopped fresh parsley

Salt and freshly ground pepper

1 tablespoon dry bread crumbs

1 tablespoon freshly grated Parmesan

Olive oil

Detach the legs and open up the crab's body. Remove and discard the stomach sac and grey appendages. Scrape out all the meat. Crack the legs and claws, and scrape out the meat. Flake all the crab meat, and set aside.

Heat the olive oil in a saucepan, add the leek, onion, carrot, and celery and sauté over medium heat for about 5 to 7 minutes, or until golden.

Add the sherry, tomatoes, and crushed chilies and cook until most of the liquid has evaporated, stirring occasionally.

Add the crab meat and parsley and cook for a further 5 minutes. Season to taste.

Preheat the oven to 400°F.

Divide the mixture and put it back into the crab shells, patting it down. Sprinkle with the bread crumbs and Parmesan cheese and drizzle a little olive oil over the top.

Brown in the hot oven for about 15 minutes or under a hot broiler, and serve hot.

VEAL KIDNEYS IN ARMAGNAC AND CREAM
Rognons de veau à l'Armagnac

 Preparation
25 minutes

Cooking
20 minutes   **Serves 4**

This dish also works well with lambs' kidneys, which are more readily available.

1½ pounds veal kidneys (about 2 large ones)

⅓ cup butter

¼ cup peanut oil

½ pound button mushrooms, thinly sliced

½ cup finely chopped shallots

¼ cup Armagnac

½ cup dry white wine

1 tablespoon Dijon-style mustard

⅔ cup heavy or whipping cream (or crème fraîche)

Salt and freshly ground pepper

Fresh parsley finely chopped

Cut the kidneys into slices, removing the core and any fat.

Melt half the butter and half the oil in a large, heavy skillet. When it is hot, add the kidneys and toss for about 4 to 5 minutes, until they are sealed. Empty the kidneys into a strainer and leave to drain for 5 minutes.

Heat the rest of the butter and oil in the pan, add the mushrooms and shallots, and sauté for about 3 to 4 minutes, then return the kidneys to the pan. Heat the Armagnac in a ladle over high heat until it flames and pour this over the kidneys.

When the flames die down, add the white wine, stir, and cook all the ingredients together for about 3 minutes. Season to taste.

Mix the mustard and cream or crème fraîche together, add to the pan, and cook over medium heat for a further 3 to 4 minutes, stirring occasionally.

Scatter the parsley over the top and serve.

Serve with mashed potatoes to soak up the sauce.

SALAD WITH GARLIC CROUTONS
Salade avec croûtons à l'ail

Preparation
20 minutes

Serves 4

About ¾ pound mixed green salad leaves

Slightly stale small French baguette

2 garlic cloves

2 tablespoons walnut oil

2 tablespoons olive oil

1 tablespoon chopped fresh herbs
(such as parsley and chives) for sprinkling

For the dressing:

⅓ cup walnut oil

1 tablespoon red wine vinegar

2 garlic cloves, crushed

Salt and freshly ground pepper to taste

Wash and dry the salad leaves and place them in a large salad bowl.

Cut the small French baguette in half lengthwise and rub with the garlic cloves. Then cut the bread into small squares.

Heat the combined oils in a skillet and sauté the pieces of bread over high heat for about 3 to 4 minutes, or until golden-brown, stirring all the time. Take care not to burn them.

Remove from the pan with a slotted spoon and scatter the croûtons over the salad.

To make the dressing, combine oil, vinegar, crushed garlic, salt, and pepper, and pour it over the salad just before serving. Sprinkle with the fresh chopped herbs.

CATALAN SALAD
Salade Catalane

Preparation
15 minutes

Serves 4 to 6

About ¾ pound mixed green salad leaves

3 large tomatoes, quartered

1 large red onion or 8 scallions, finely sliced

1 green bell pepper, cored, seeded, and thinly sliced

1 large slice raw ham (Bayonne or Parma), cut into fine strips

1 cup black olives

3 medium-size hard-boiled eggs, quartered

For the dressing:

½ cup olive oil

2 tablespoons sherry vinegar

3 garlic cloves, finely chopped

Salt and freshly ground pepper

1 tablespoon finely chopped fresh parsley

Wash and dry the salad leaves and place in a large bowl or platter.

Add the tomatoes, onion(s), and green pepper. Top with the strips of ham, black olives, and quartered eggs.

Combine the oil, vinegar, garlic, salt, pepper, and parsley; pour over the salad just before serving. Toss and serve.

ROAST LAMB FROM PAULLIAC
Agneau rôti de Paulliac

 Preparation
30 minutes

Cooking
1½ hours   Serves 4 to 6

1 leg of lamb (3½ to 4 pounds)

8 garlic cloves, peeled

⅓ cup softened butter

1½ cups fresh bread crumbs (see page 25)

1 fresh thyme sprig, crumbled

½ cup finely chopped fresh parsley

2 tablespoons olive oil

Salt and freshly ground pepper

Make slits in the leg of lamb and insert slivers of garlic cut from 2 of the cloves.

Preheat the oven to 400°F.

In a small bowl, mix the butter, bread crumbs, remaining garlic cloves, crushed, and the thyme and parsley, into a paste, using a fork. Season with salt and pepper to taste.

Oil a large roasting pan and put in the lamb. Pat half the bread crumb mixture over one side of the joint and roast for about 45 minutes.

Remove the lamb from the oven, turn it over, and pat on the rest of the mixture. Return to the oven and continue roasting for about another 30 to 45 minutes. To stop the juices in the pan burning, add a few spoonfuls of water every now and again.

Take the lamb out of the oven and let it rest for 5 minutes before carving.

Place the leg of lamb on a warmed platter and serve with the juices from the pan.

Serve with green beans or potatoes au gratin.

SALAD WITH ROQUEFORT AND WALNUTS
Salade au Roquefort et aux noix

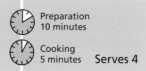

Preparation
15 minutes

Serves 4

About ¾ pound mixed salad leaves
(such as lambs lettuce, oak leaf, lollo rosso, butter lettuce, etc.)

¼ pound Roquefort cheese

1 cup halved or quartered walnuts

For the dressing:

⅓ cup walnut oil

1 tablespoon red wine vinegar

Salt and freshly ground pepper

Wash and dry the salad leaves
and place in a salad bowl.

Crumble the cheese and add to
the salad leaves.

To make the dressing, combine
the oil, vinegar, and seasoning to
taste. Pour the dressing over the
lettuce just before serving and
toss.

Serve with the walnuts scattered
on top.

SALAD OF DANDELION AND BACON
Salade de pissenlits et petits lardons

Preparation
10 minutes

Cooking
5 minutes

Serves 4

About ¾ cup dandelion leaves or chicory

Salt and freshly ground pepper

1 garlic clove, chopped

1 tablespoon goose, pork, or chicken fat

6 thin bacon slices, cut into small strips

1 tablespoon red wine vinegar

Wash and dry the salad leaves
and put them in a bowl.

Sprinkle a little salt, pepper, and
chopped garlic on top.

In a skillet, heat the fat and fry
the bacon strips. When they are
crispy, empty the contents of the
skillet over the salad.

Off the heat, pour the vinegar
into the hot pan, swirl it around
quickly, and also pour over the
salad.

Toss and serve immediately.

DUCK BREAST WITH GARLIC SAUCE
Magrets de canard à l'aillade Toulousaine

Preparation 30 minutes
Marinate 2 hours

Cooking 15 minutes
Serves 4

2 duck breasts (¾ pound each)

2 garlic cloves, chopped

½ cup Armagnac

2 fresh thyme sprigs

Salt and freshly ground pepper

3 tablespoons goose fat
or
2 tablespoons butter with 1 tablespoon oil

For the sauce (aillade):

¾ cup shelled walnuts

3 garlic cloves, peeled

2 tablespoons iced water

⅔ cup extra virgin olive oil

1 tablespoon finely chopped fresh parsley

Salt and freshly ground pepper

In a bowl, combine the chopped garlic, Armagnac, fresh thyme leaves, salt and pepper. Add the duck breasts and coat them with the mixture. Leave to marinate for about 2 hours, turning occasionally.

To prepare the sauce (aillade), combine walnuts, garlic cloves and the iced water in a blender or food processor. Blend until the mixture is smooth and creamy (add a little more iced water if necessary). Then, with the machine running, pour in the oil very slowly, as for a mayonnaise. Add the chopped parsley and season to taste.

Drain the duck breasts, reserving the marinade. With a sharp knife, make 3 or 4 slits on the skins of each breast.

In a skillet, heat the goose fat, or butter and oil, and cook the breasts, skin-side down first, for 6 to 8 minutes, then for 5 minutes on the other side, or until the meat is cooked but still pink inside. Remove the duck breasts from the skillet and keep warm in a low oven.

Strain the reserved marinade and pour into the skillet. Boil for 1 to 2 minutes.

Slice the duck breasts, place on a hot serving dish, and pour the sauce over. Serve immediately, accompanied by the aillade and a green salad.

GOAT'S CHEESE SALAD
Salade au fromage de chèvre

 Preparation 10 minutes Marinate 2 hours
Cooking 5 minutes **Serves 6**

1 pound mixed salad leaves (such as chicory, radicchio, oak leaves, etc.)

Fresh chives, chopped

6 slices (about ½ inch thick) goat's cheese

3 to 4 rosemary sprigs

Olive oil to cover the slices of cheese

6 slices of white bread, slightly larger than the cheese slices

For the dressing:

⅓ cup olive oil

1 tablespoon red wine vinegar

1 garlic cloves, crushed

Salt and freshly ground pepper

Wash and dry the salad and put in a bowl with the chives.

Place the slices of cheese in a dish, cover them with the rosemary sprigs and olive oil. Leave to marinate for about 2 hours or overnight.

Preheat the broiler.

Toast the slices of bread. Remove the slices of cheese from the marinade and place each one on a piece of toast. Do not remove any pieces of rosemary adhering to the cheese. Broil the cheese until it is hot and bubbling.

Meanwhile, make the dressing. Mix the olive oil, vinegar, garlic, salt, and pepper. Pour this over the salad, toss well, and divide the salad between 6 plates.

Take the cheese toasts from under the broiler and place on top of each plate of salad. Serve immediately.

FOIE GRAS SALAD
Salade au foie gras

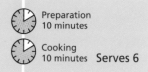 Preparation 10 minutes
Cooking 10 minutes **Serves 6**

If you have fresh truffles, you can add some thin slices to this salad, or, if you have some duck or pork confit, add a few pieces to each helping.

1 pound French green beans

1 pound asparagus tips

1 pound chicory leaves

½ pound foie gras, cut in 6 slices

For the dressing:

⅓ cup vegetable oil

2 tablespoons red wine vinegar

Salt and freshly ground pepper

Either steam or boil the French beans and asparagus separately. They should not be overcooked and should remain crisp. Immediately after cooking, refresh the vegetables under running cold water and drain.

Wash and dry the salad leaves and place in a bowl. Add the cooked asparagus tips and green beans and toss. Divide between 6 plates.

Place 1 slice of foie gras on top of each plate.

To make the dressing, combine the oil, vinegar, salt, and pepper, and just before serving, spoon the dressing over each plate.

BOURRIDE OF MONKFISH FROM SETE

Bourride de lotte à la Sètoise

Preparation 30 minutes

Cooking 30 minutes

Serves 4

Bourride is one of the great fish dishes of the South of France. There are many ways of making it, but the main characteristic is that some of the stock in which the fish has been cooked is added to a garlic-flavored mayonnaise called Aïoli, to make a wonderfully smooth, pale sauce to be served with the fish.

2½ pounds monkfish

¼ pound chard or spinach leaves, stems removed

¼ cup olive oil

2 leeks, white part only, thinly sliced

2 medium-size onions, chopped

2 medium-size carrots, peeled and chopped

1¼ cups white wine

Salt and freshly ground pepper

For the sauce (Aïoli):

6 garlic cloves, peeled

½ teaspoon strong Dijon-style mustard

4 medium-size egg yolks

Salt and pepper

1¼ cups olive oil

Skin and bone the fish, or buy ready-prepared, and cut it into chunks.

Wash the chard or spinach and slice in thin strips.

Heat the oil in a large skillet and stir in the leeks, onions and carrots, and the chard or spinach. Cover and sweat over medium-low heat for 5 minutes.

Add the fish and let some of the liquid evaporate before pouring in the white wine. Season to taste and cook over medium-high heat for 15 minutes, or until the fish is cooked but still firm.

Meanwhile, prepare the sauce. Crush the garlic cloves through a press and place in a bowl. Add the mustard, egg yolks, salt and pepper to taste, and mix well. Then add the oil, a drop at a time at first, then in a thin stream, beating constantly, as for a mayonnaise, until quite firm.

Remove the fish from the pan and keep hot in a serving dish. Slowly stir a little of the hot cooking liquid into the aïoli, then gradually pour it all back into the pan. Stirring all the time, thicken the sauce over very low heat.

Pour the sauce over the fish and serve immediately with boiled or steamed baby potatoes.

GREEN PEAS WITH HAM
Petits pois au jambon

 Preparation
30 minutes

Cooking
25 minutes   **Serves 6**

¼ pound smoked ham, chopped or cubed

¼ cup goose fat or butter

2 pounds fresh, shelled green peas,
or
2 pounds frozen peas

10 small pearl onions, whole and peeled (see page 24)
or
15 to 20 scallions, whites only

2 tablespoons water or stock

Salt and freshly ground pepper

1 bouquet garni of thyme, parsley, and 1 bay leaf

Melt the goose fat or butter in a skillet and gently sauté the ham over medium heat for 3 to 4 minutes.

Add the peas, onions, water or stock. Season with salt and pepper and add the bouquet garni. Stir well and cover the pan firmly, in order to retain the moisture.

Reduce the heat and cook gently for about 20 minutes, or until the peas are tender.

Check the seasoning and remove the bouquet garni before serving.

RED CABBAGE WITH CHESTNUTS
Chou rouge aux marrons

 Preparation
30 minutes

 Cooking
1 hour   **Serves 4**

1 red cabbage (1½ to 2 pounds)

2 tablespoons goose fat or butter

1 pound fresh chestnuts, peeled (see page 24)
or
1 pound whole canned or vacuum-packed chesnuts
(allow less cooking time)

Salt and freshly ground pepper

Wash the red cabbage and cut it into quarters. Remove the core and then cut each quarter into thick slices.

In a casserole, melt the goose fat or butter, add the cabbage, chestnuts, salt and pepper. Cover and cook *very* slowly for about 1 hour, stirring occasionally. (If using canned chestnuts, add them to the casserole for the last half hour only).

As the cabbage cooks only in its own juices and the fat, check that it does not stick to the bottom of the casserole.

This dish is even more delicious when re-heated the following day.

PYRENEAN TROUT
La truite des Pyrénées

Preparation
25 minutes

Cooking
15 minutes   Serves 4

Pastis is an aniseed-flavored apéritif which is very popular in the South of France. Pernod is an acceptable alternative but, if you do not like the taste of aniseed, you can use a dry vermouth instead.

4 medium-size trout, cleaned

About ½ cup all-purpose flour

Salt and freshly ground pepper

1 cup clarified butter (see page 25)

¾ pound small mushrooms, thinly sliced

1 small garlic clove, peeled and chopped

¼ cup pastis

1¼ cups heavy or whipping cream

Mix the flour with salt and pepper, then roll the trout in the seasoned flour and shake off any excess.

Heat ¾ cup of the clarified butter in a non-stick skillet and cook the trout for 5 minutes on each side over moderate heat.

Remove the trout and keep them warm in a very low oven.

Turn up the heat under the pan and cook the mushrooms and garlic in the remaining clarified butter. Add the pastis, let it bubble, then add the cream. Stir well and cook to form a smooth sauce.

To serve, put each trout on a plate and spoon over some of the sauce.

Serve with steamed or boiled new potatoes.

MUSHROOMS WITH GARLIC AND PARSLEY
Cèpes à la Bordelaise

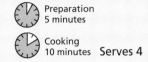

Preparation 5 minutes

Cooking 10 minutes Serves 4

Cèpes are expensive wild mushrooms and are seldom found fresh in the U.S. So instead you can use button, field, or shiitake mushrooms.

2 pounds fresh cèpes or other full-flavored mushrooms

½ cup olive oil

Salt and freshly ground pepper

2 garlic cloves, chopped

2 tablespoons finely chopped parsley

Wipe the cèpes, or other mushrooms, with a dry cloth or paper towels (do not wash them) to remove any earth. Cut off the stalks, set aside, and slice the caps.

Heat the oil in a skillet and when hot, add the sliced caps of the cèpes or other mushrooms. Brown them on both sides over low heat, and season to taste.

Chop the stalks, and mix them with the garlic and parsley. Sprinkle this over the caps and stir well. Sauté together for 3 to 5 minutes over medium-low heat.

Serve at once.

POTATOES SARLAT STYLE
Pommes à la Sarladaise

Preparation 15 minutes

Cooking 25 minutes Serves 4 to 6

2 pounds medium-size potatoes

½ cup goose fat

6 garlic cloves, chopped

2 tablespoons chopped parsley

Salt and freshly ground pepper

Wash and peel the potatoes. Cut them into ⅓-inch slices.

Melt three-quarters of the goose fat in a large non-stick skillet. Add the potatoes and stir them in the fat for 5 minutes. Cover and cook over low heat for 15 to 20 minutes, or until the potatoes are cooked through, stirring occasionally. Take care not to break the potatoes when stirring.

Remove the cover, turn up the heat, add the remaining goose fat, the chopped garlic and parsley mixed together, and season to taste. Shake the pan over the heat for 2 to 3 minutes and serve while hot.

SALMIS OF PIGEON
Salmis de palombes

 Preparation
20 minutes

Cooking
2 hours   Serves 4

Salmis is a stew and in the Basque region, it is made with palombes. The palombe is a kind of pigeon only found in the South-West of France, but squab is a good substitute.

2 squab

4 tablespoons butter

½ cup finely chopped bacon

2 medium-size onions, finely chopped

2 carrots, finely chopped

¼ cup Armagnac

2 level tablespoons all-purpose flour

2½ cups red wine

1¼ cups chicken, veal, or beef stock

Bouquet garni of thyme, parsley, and 1 bay leaf

Salt and freshly ground pepper

Slices of fried bread to garnish

Cut the squab in half. Heat the butter in a large pan and brown them on both sides for approximately 4 to 5 minutes.

Remove the squab from the pan and add the bacon, onions, and carrots, and fry until golden. Return the squab to the pan. Heat the Armagnac in a ladle over a low flame until it lights and pour it over the squab.

When the flames have died down, sprinkle the flour over, stir round until all the juices have been absorbed.

Slowly pour over the wine and stock, stir to mix well. Add the bouquet garni, salt and pepper to taste, and bring to a boil. Turn down the heat and simmer very gently for about 1½ hours, or until the squab are tender.

Remove the squab and keep them warm in a low oven, covered with foil.

Remove the bouquet garni, tip all the sauce and vegetables into the blender, and liquidize until smooth.*

Put the squab back in the pan. Pour the sauce through a strainer, pressing all the liquid through, and pour over the squab. Reheat and cook for a

further 15 to 20 minutes.

Serve the squab on a platter, cover with the sauce, and garnish with triangles of fried bread.

(*) Note: If the sauce is too thin, cook it rapidly over high heat to reduce it before returning the squab to the pan.

STUFFED EGGPLANT
Aubergines farçies

Preparation 10 minutes   Refrigerate overnight

Cooking 1 hour   Serves 6

3 long eggplants

1 scant cup olive oil

3 large tomatoes

3½ cups fresh bread crumbs (see page 25)

1¼ cups milk

3 large garlic cloves, crushed

4 tablespoons finely chopped parsley

4 scallions, white and green parts, finely chopped

¾ cup finely chopped fresh fennel stalks and fronds

Salt and freshly ground pepper

½ cup dry bread crumbs

Olive oil to sprinkle

Cut the eggplants in half lengthwise. Salt them and leave to drain for about 20 minutes, then rinse and dry them. Make two shallow slits, lengthwise, in the flesh of each eggplant. Fry them in the olive oil for about 4 minutes, turning them occasionally. Leave them aside to cool.

When cool, scrape the flesh from the skins with a spoon and put the skins side by side in a baking dish.

Cut the tomatoes in half, crosswise, seed and place them beside the eggplant skins.

Soak the fresh bread crumbs in the milk for 5 minutes, then squeeze out the milk with your hands and put the bread crumbs in a bowl.

Finely chop the eggplant flesh and add, together with the garlic, parsley, scallions, and fennel to the bread crumbs and mix together thoroughly. Season with salt and pepper.

Preheat the oven to 400°F.

Fill the eggplant skins and tomato halves with the mixture, patting into shape. Sprinkle over the dry bread crumbs and a little olive oil. Bake in a hot oven for about 30 minutes.

The stuffing should be nice and brown on top and can be finished off under a hot broiler before serving.

BRAISED PORK WITH CHESTNUTS
Porc aux chataignes

 Preparation
40 minutes

Cooking
2½ hours

Serves 5 to 6

Fresh chestnuts are seasonal, but peeled, canned or vacuum-packed chestnuts are available all year round. They will need less cooking time than the fresh ones. Chestnuts can be used in a variety of ways, savoury and sweet, roasted, boiled, puréed, or candied as marrons glacés.

2¼ pounds pork (leg preferably), boned, and prepared for roasting

3 tablespoons pork dripping or butter

20 small pearl onions, peeled (see page 24)

3 garlic cloves, chopped

2¼ cups dry white wine

Salt and freshly ground pepper

35 to 40 fresh chestnuts, peeled (see page 24)
or
35 to 40 canned or vacuum-packed chestnuts

Preheat the oven to 325°F.

Melt the pork dripping or butter in a heavy flameproof casserole with a tight-fitting lid. Brown the meat on all sides for about 15 to 20 minutes.

Add the onions and gently brown them, then add the garlic and the wine. Allow to bubble, then turn the heat down. Add salt and pepper to taste and cook gently for approximately 5 minutes. Cover the casserole and put in the pre-heated oven for about 1½ to 2 hours.

If you are using fresh chestnuts, add them to the casserole for the last 45 minutes of cooking. If they are canned or vacuum-packed, add them for the last 15 minutes of cooking only.

Transfer the meat to a heated serving dish, place the onions and the chestnuts around the meat. Serve the cooking juices separately.

Serve with Brussels sprouts or cabbage.

JERUSALEM ARTICHOKE FRITTERS
Beignets de topinambours

Preparation
25 minutes

Cooking
45 minutes

Serves 4

As Jerusalem artichokes (or sunchokes) are not always available, these fritters can be made with pieces or slices of other pre-cooked vegetables such as celeriac, zucchini, or eggplant as an alternative.

1 pound Jerusalem artichokes, well washed and peeled
Vegetable oil for frying

For the batter:

1 good cup all-purpose flour
1 whole medium-size egg
Scant ¼ cup oil
Salt and freshly ground pepper
⅔ cup milk
1 medium-size egg white

Cook the artichokes in salted, boiling water for about 10 to 20 minutes (depending on their size), or until just tender (you can check by piercing them with the point of a knife). Drain, cool and cut them into thick slices.

To make the batter, sift the flour into a mixing bowl, make a well in the center and add the whole egg, the oil, salt, and pepper and mix to a smooth cream, adding the milk a little at a time. When the batter is smooth and thick, stop adding the milk; it should be thicker than a pancake batter. **Leave to rest for 1 hour.**

Just before using the batter, beat the egg white until stiff and fold it carefully into the batter.

Heat the oil and, when it is hot, but not smoking, drop several slices of artichoke into the batter. Then dip them, one by one, into the hot oil, using either tongs, a metal skewer or a fork. Cook for 2 to 3 minutes, or until puffed and golden-brown, turning them once. Remove from the oil with a slotted spoon and drain on paper towels.

Place in a warm oven (350°F) while you cook the rest.

Repeat with the remaining slices (a few at a time to avoid sticking together).

RABBIT WITH PRUNES
Lapin aux pruneaux

Preparation
15 minutes

Cooking
2 hours

Serves 4

The best prunes come from Agen in South-West France and are used both in sweet and savoury dishes. California also produces excellent prunes.

1 rabbit (3 to 3½ pounds), cut into pieces
or
8 to 10 rabbit pieces

2 cups red wine

1 tablespoon superfine sugar

20 Agen or Californian prunes

Salt and freshly ground pepper

2 tablespoons vegetable oil

¼ cup Armagnac

1 tablespoon fresh thyme leaves

1 medium-size onion, finely chopped

2 garlic cloves, finely chopped

3 shallots, finely chopped

⅔ cup heavy or whipping cream (or crème fraîche)

Mix the red wine and sugar in a saucepan and bring to a boil. When the sugar has dissolved, add the prunes and simmer for 10 to 15 minutes, stirring occasionally. Remove from the heat, cover the pan, and leave aside for 10 minutes. Strain and reserve the liquid, keeping the prunes in the pan.

Season the rabbit pieces with salt and pepper. Heat the oil in a large non-stick sauté pan and lightly brown the rabbit pieces on all sides (for about 15 minutes), then remove from the heat.

Heat the Armagnac in a ladle over a flame until alight, then pour over the rabbit pieces. Swirl gently until the flames have died down.

Put the pan back over medium-low heat, add the fresh thyme leaves, onion, garlic, and shallots. Cook, stirring all the time, for a further 5 minutes.

Stir in the wine reserved from the prunes and bring to a boil. Then cover, reduce the heat, and simmer gently for 40 to 45 minutes.)

Remove from the heat, place the rabbit pieces on a dish, and keep warm in a moderate oven (325°F).

Reduce the liquid in the pan over high heat until thicker and almost syrupy. Add the cream

and, stirring all the time, bring to a boil for 2 to 3 minutes, until the sauce is smooth.

Return the rabbit pieces to the pan, add the prunes, and reheat for 2 to 3 minutes, stirring.

Place the rabbit pieces and prunes on a heated serving dish. Pour the sauce over and serve immediately.

BASQUE CHICKEN
Poulet basquaise

  Preparation
30 minutes

Cooking
1 hour 15 mins **Serves 4 to 6**

1 chicken (4½ pounds), cut into 8 pieces
or
8 chicken pieces

Scant ½ cup olive oil

2 large onions, peeled

3 red bell peppers

2 green bell peppers

3 garlic cloves, peeled and crushed

½ teaspoon dried crushed chilies

1 pound ripe tomatoes, peeled (see page 24), seeded, and chopped
or
1 large can (28 ounces) tomatoes, chopped

⅔ cup dry white wine

Salt and freshly ground pepper

½ pound unsmoked ham, cubed

½ cup pitted black olives

Thinly slice the onions. Seed the green and red bell peppers, and cut them into strips.

Heat ¼ cup of the olive oil in a deep skillet, add the chicken pieces and brown them over moderate heat for about 5 to 6 minutes on each side.

Remove the chicken pieces and place them in a flameproof casserole.

In a separate pan, heat the remaining olive oil, add the onions and peppers, and cook gently for 10 minutes, stirring occasionally. Add the crushed garlic cloves, dried crushed chilies, tomatoes, white wine, salt and pepper to taste, and cook for a further 15 minutes, stirring occasionally, or until the vegetables are very soft and form a rich sauce.

Preheat the oven to 375°F.

Pour this sauce over the chicken pieces in the casserole, cover, and place in the oven. Cook for about 30 to 40 minutes or until the chicken is tender.

Add the cubed ham and cook for a further 5 minutes.

Remove the casserole from the oven, transfer to a large serving dish, and garnish with black olives.

Serve with a fresh green salad and some hot French bread.

TRUFFLE OMELET
Omelette aux truffes

Preparation 10 minutes

Cooking 5 minutes

Refrigerate 2 hours

Serves 2

The famous black truffles in the Périgord, Tuber Melanosporum or "black diamonds," are known for their outstanding aroma and taste. If you are unable to get the "real thing," however, you can buy preserved truffles in tins or glass jars.

If you are able to find (and afford!) a real truffle, you can preserve it for months by putting it in a screwtop jar and covering it with equal parts of port and Armagnac. You can use the liquid, perfumed by the truffle, to flavor pâtés or other dishes, but remember to keep topping up the liquid in the jar.

| 1 medium truffle, about 2 ounces |
| 4 large eggs |
| Salt and freshly ground pepper |
| 4 tablespoons butter |

Scrub and dry the truffle.

Cut it into thin rounds and then into matchsticks.

Break the eggs into a bowl, add the truffle, cover, and leave in the refrigerator for about 2 hours.

To make the omelet, beat the eggs with a fork and add salt and pepper to taste. Heat the butter in an omelet pan and when hot but not burnt, pour in the eggs and stir round to mix in the butter for a few seconds.

When the omelet has almost set, slide it on to a hot serving dish and, using the pan, fold it in two.

Serve at once.

BOILED CHICKEN LANGUEDOC STYLE
Poule au pot de Toulouse

Preparation
20 minutes

Cooking
3 hours

Serves 6

This dish can be found throughout France cooked in various ways. Ideally, it should be made with a boiling fowl (also called hen or stewing chicken) and cooked for much longer, but nowadays, old-fashioned boiling fowl are difficult to find, so replace with chicken.

1 chicken (4½ pounds), with giblets, including liver
Salt and freshly ground pepper
⅓ cup milk
2 cups fresh white bread, crust removed, cut into pieces
4 garlic cloves
Scant ½ pound Bayonne or Parma ham
¼ cup chopped parsley
½ teaspoon freshly grated nutmeg
2 medium-size eggs
2 medium-size onions
6 cloves
2 medium-size carrots, peeled and sliced
2 celery stalks, cut into chunks
16 white and black peppercorns
Bouquet garni: parsley, thyme, and 1 bay leaf

Firstly, remove the giblets and liver and set aside. Season the chicken with salt and pepper inside and out.

Heat the milk in a saucepan and add the bread. Stir with a wooden spoon until it forms a paste. Leave to cool.

Finely chop 2 garlic cloves. In a food processor, finely chop the ham and the chicken liver. If you are using frozen poultry liver, make sure you pat it dry with paper towels after defrosting and before chopping it in the food processor.

Put the chopped ham and liver in a bowl. Add the garlic, soaked bread, parsley, salt, pepper, and nutmeg, and mix together well with a wooden spoon. In a small bowl, beat the two eggs and add to the stuffing mixture. Blend together well.

Stuff the chicken with the mixture and sew up the opening with a needle and thick thread.

Peel the onions and stud them with the cloves.

Pour 6 pints of water into a pot or casserole large enough to contain the chicken. Add the giblets, carrots, onions, celery, remaining 2 garlic cloves, the peppercorns and bouquet garni.

Bring to a boil and add the chicken. Stir and season to taste with salt and pepper. Cover and

cook over very low heat for 2½ to 3 hours.

Remove the chicken from the pot, carve it, and put the pieces on a serving dish with the stuffing. Pour over a little of the cooking liquid and serve.

If you are using the cooking broth as a soup, strain it into a tureen and serve as a starter.

ENTRECOTE STEAK WITH MARROW AND SHALLOTS
Entrecôte Bordelaise

Preparation
15 minutes

Cooking
30 minutes

Serves 3 to 4

Entrecôte is not always easy to find outside France. Sirloin (a cut between faux-filet and rumpsteak) or boneless rib steak can be used instead. Marrow bones are also difficult to find, but the Bordelaise sauce is just as delicious without.

1 thick entrecôte or sirloin steak (2 pounds)
or
2 steaks (1 pound each)

1 marrow bone, giving about ¼ pound of marrow

4 tablespoons unsalted butter

¾ cup finely chopped shallots

⅔ cup red wine

10 white peppercorns, crushed

½ cup rich veal or chicken stock

Salt

1 tablespoon vegetable oil

2 tablespoons chopped fresh parsley

If you have access to a marrow bone, ask the butcher to saw the bone into approximately 3-inch sections. Plunge the bones into a pan of lightly salted boiling water. Bring the water back to a boil, reduce the heat, and simmer, uncovered, for 5 minutes. Lift out the bones and, using a towel to protect your hand, sharply shake the bones on a board until the marrow slides out. Set aside on paper towels to drain.

To prepare the sauce, melt the butter in a saucepan, add the shallots and cook gently for 2 to 3 minutes.

Add the red wine, crushed peppercorns, and bring to a boil. Reduce the sauce by one-third, then add the stock and let it cook over low heat for 15 to 20 minutes. Season to taste with salt and keep hot over very low heat.

Brush your steak(s) with oil and lightly sprinkle with salt on both sides. Cook under a very hot broiler or on an iron grill pan to your taste – rare, medium or well done. Cut the meat into thick slices and arrange on a heated serving dish.

Cut the marrow into cubes and stir into the hot shallot sauce for 1 to 2 minutes, then quickly pour the sauce over the meat. Sprinkle with the chopped parsley and serve immediately with French fries.

PEELING TOMATOES

Using a pointed knife, make an incision in the shape of a cross on the base of each tomato.

Plunge the tomatoes in a pan of boiling water without crowding them, making sure they are totally immersed.

Count 10 seconds and remove them from the pan.

Leave the tomatoes to cool, then peel off the skin.

Cut the tomatoes in half crosswise and using a small teaspoon, scoop out the seeds.

PEELING BELL PEPPERS

Brush the peppers with olive oil, using a pastry brush.

Place the peppers on a baking sheet and bake in a preheated oven (400°F) for 30 to 40 minutes.

Remove the peppers from the oven and place in a plastic bag. Tie up the bag to keep the steam in and leave the peppers to sweat for about 15 minutes, or until they are cool enough to handle. The skin will then peel off easily.

PEELING ONIONS

Plunge the onions in a pan of boiling water without crowding them, and leave for 2 minutes.

Remove the onions from the boiling water and then plunge them into cold water.

Pull off the skin and trim the ends.

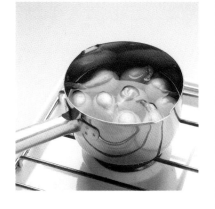

PEELING CHESTNUTS

With the point of a knife, make a slit in the flat sides of the chestnuts and boil them for 3 to 4 minutes.

While the chestnuts are still warm, remove the shells and inner skins, using a sharp knife. If any of the inner skins are difficult to remove, reboil the chestnuts for a few seconds.

JELLIED CHICKEN STOCK

2 pounds chicken wings, drumsticks, and leftover carcass of roast chicken

1 tablespoon chicken fat or butter

2 large onions, coarsely chopped

1 large carrot, peeled and coarsely chopped

1 celery stalk, coarsely chopped

Bouquet garni: parsley, thyme, and 1 bay leaf or 3 parsley sprigs

½ teaspoon salt

Pepper to taste

3¾ pints water

In a large pan, melt the fat or butter. Fry the chopped onions until golden-brown, about 10 minutes.

Add the chicken pieces and carcass, the carrot, celery, bouquet garni, salt and pepper, and add the water. The water must cover the chicken.

Cover the pan, bring to a boil, turn down the heat, and simmer for 2 hours, stirring occasionally, by which time the liquid should have reduced by half.

Pour the stock through a colander into a large bowl and leave to cool for 15 minutes, then remove the fat that has risen to the surface using a spoon.

Strain a second time through a fine-mesh strainer lined with cheesecloth or paper towels.

Place in the refrigerator until it has set into a jelly.

Before using the jellied stock, remove any trace of fat that may cloud the surface.

CLARIFIED BUTTER

Melt the butter in a small saucepan and heat gently without allowing it to color.

Skim off the foam as it rises to the top, leaving the milk solids to sink to the bottom of the pan.

Slowly pour the clear butter into a bowl through a strainer lined with cheesecloth or paper towels. Leave to settle for 10 minutes, then pour it into another bowl, leaving any remaining sediment behind.

Allow the clarified butter to cool and keep it in a jar in the refrigerator until needed.

Clarified butter will keep longer than normal butter.

FRESH BREAD CRUMBS

Take a loaf of white bread at least 4 days old. Remove all the crust and cut into 1-inch cubes.

Place a few cubes of bread at a time in a food processor and, using the metal blade, process until the bread is reduced to crumbs.

Repeat with the remaining cubes.

Any crumbs that are not needed immediately can be put into a plastic bag or small container and frozen.